khost

PROVINCIAL HANDBOOK / A Guide to the People and the Province

Khost

Roads —
District Border - - -
River —
Provincial Center ⊙
City ●

LOWER ELEVATION — HIGHER ELEVATION

Pakistan

Paktya

Paktika

Zazi Maidan

Zazi Maidan

Bak

Bak

Terezai (Ali Sher)

Ali Sher

Ali Sher

Khost (Matun)

Sabari (Yaqubi)

Kholbesat

Yaqubi

Khost City

Sheikh Amir

Sheikh Amir

Gurbuz

Musa Khel

Musa Khel

Qalandar

Khost Mela

Dadwal

Mando Zai

Dragai

Dragai

Tanai

Nadar Shah Kot

Nadar Shah Kot

Shamat (Dwamonda)

Spera

Spera

Spera

Table of Contents

List of Tables and Maps

Cover Photo by: Frances Fierst
Title Page Photo by: Rahmatullah Kawsar

Acronyms and Key Terms

ABP	Afghan Border Police
ADT	Agribusiness Development Team
ANA	Afghan National Army
ANBP	Afghan National Border Police
ANDS	Afghan National Development Strategy
ANP	Afghan National Police
ANSF	Afghan National Security Forces
Arbakai	A volunteer, tribal police force which follows a strict ethical code
AWCC	Afghan Wireless Communication Company
BEFA	Basic Education for Afghanistan
BPHS	Basic Package of Health Services
CA	Civil Affairs
CDCs	Community Development Councils
CERP	Commander's Emergency Response Program
CHC	Comprehensive Health Centers
COIN	Counter Insurgency
CSO	Central Statistics Office
DDS	District Development Shuras
DIAG	Disbandment of Illegal Armed Groups
DoS	US Department of State
DST	District Support Team
FATA	Federally Administered Tribal Areas
GIRoA	Government of the Islamic Republic of Afghanistan
HIG or HIH	Hezb-e Islami Gulbuddin ("Islamic Party" formed by Gulbuddin Hekmatyar)

HIK	Hezb-e Islami Khalis ("Islamic Party" formed by Mohammad Yunus Khalis)
ICRC	International Committee of the Red Cross
IDLG	Independent Directorate for Local Governance
IED	Improvised Explosive Devices
IO	International Organization
IRoA	Islamic Republic of Afghanistan
ISAF	International Security Assistance Force
ISI	Inter-Service Intelligence (Pakistan)
Karez	A small underground irrigation system popular in Afghanistan
LGCD	Local Governance and Community Development Program
Meshrano Jirga	Elders' Assembly, upper house of Afghan National Assembly
MRRD	Ministry of Rural Rehabilitation and Development
Mustafiat	Department of Finance
NDS	National Directorate for Security
NGO	Non-Governmental Organization
NSP	National Solidarity Program
NWFP	North West Frontier Province
Pashtunwali	The Pashtuns' pre-Islamic code of conduct
PC	Provincial Council
PDC	Provincial Development Council
PDP	Provincial Development Plan
PRT	Provincial Reconstruction Team
UN	United Nations
UNAMA	United Nations Assistance Mission in Afghanistan
UNOPS	United Nations Office for Project Services
USACE	US Army Corp of Engineers
USAID	US Agency for International Development
USDA	US Department of Agriculture
Wali	Governor
Wolesi Jirga	People's Assembly, lower house of Afghan National Assembly
Woluswal	District Administrator

Guide to the Handbook

This handbook is a concise field guide to Khost for internationals deploying to the province. Field personnel have used these guides in Afghanistan since June 2008 to accelerate their orientation process and to serve as a refresher on different aspects of the province during their tour.

Reading this book will provide a basic understanding of the people, places, history, culture, politics, economy, needs, and ideas of Khost. Building upon this understanding can help you:

- Build rapport and a regular dialogue with local leaders,

- Plan and implement pragmatic strategies (security, political, economic) to address sources of instability,

- Influence communities to support the political process, not the insurgents, and

- Build the capacity and legitimacy of a self-sufficient Afghan government and economy.

As you read the handbook and continue your inquiry in the province, seek to understand the influential leaders and groups in your local area and what beliefs and relationships drive their behavior. Think about the sources of violence in the area and whether groups are pursuing interests in a way that promotes conflict or stability. Finally, consider how various types of activities – key leader engagement, development assistance, security operations, security assistance, or public diplomacy – can effectively influence communities to work within the political process and oppose insurgency.

SOURCES AND METHODS

These handbooks are not intended as original academic research but as concise, readable summaries for practitioners in the field. The editorial team relies on its collective field experience and knowledge of the province as well as key sources such as the official Islamic Republic of Afghanistan (IRoA), United Nations and United States Government (USG) publications, and those sources listed in the appendix.

The editors made every effort to ensure accuracy. It should be noted, however, that there is often considerable disagreement regarding what is "ground truth" in Khost and things are constantly changing. As such, consider this book part of your orientation, and not an all-inclusive source for everything you need to know.

Information in this handbook is unclassified. The views and opinions expressed in this handbook are those of IDS International and in no way reflect the views of the United States Government or the United States Army.

THE ELECTRONIC UPDATE

Look for electronic updates to this book at *www.idsinternational.net/ afpakbooks*. Updates will cover new developments, issues, and leaders that emerge after publication. They will also provide corrections and expanded content in key areas based on input from readers.

We hope the handbook will continue to be a valuable tool in thinking about the challenges in Khost. If you have questions, comments, or feedback for future updates or editions please email *afpakbooks@idsinternational.net*.

ABOUT IDS INTERNATIONAL

Publisher of Afghanistan and Pakistan Provincial Handbooks Series

This book is part of a series of handbooks on Afghanistan and Pakistan provinces and regions. Afghanistan province titles include Nuristan, Kunar, Nangarhar, Laghman, Paktya, Paktika, Ghazni, Helmand, and Kandahar. Pakistan province titles include North West Frontier Province (NWFP) and the Federally Administered Tribal Areas (FATA).

In addition to publishing these handbooks, IDS International provides training and analysis to government and private organizations in the areas of politics, economics, culture, stability operations, reconstruction, counterinsurgency, and interagency relations. In particular, IDS is a leading trainer of the US military in working with Provincial Reconstruction Teams (PRTs) in Iraq and Afghanistan. IDS offers its clients expertise and experience in the difficult work of interagency collaboration in complex operations. The writers and editors on this project offer a lifetime of experience working in these provinces and share a dedication to bringing peace and prosperity to the people of Afghanistan.

Authors: Frances Fierst, Sabawoon Hanan, and Rahmatullah Kawsar

Editors: Amy Frumin and Eric Bone

Assistant Editors: Tom Viehe, Chris Hall, and Emily Rose

IDS INTERNATIONAL GOVERNMENT SERVICES

1916 Wilson Boulevard

Suite 302

Arlington, VA 22201

703-875-2212

www.idsinternational.net

afpakbooks@idsinternational.net

PUBLISHED: MAY 2010

This and other AfPak handbooks may be purchased in either hard copy or digital format. Samples are available upon request. IDS International is also a leading provider of training and support on the cultural, political, economic, interagency and information aspects of conflict. For inquires, please email *afpakbooks@idsinternational.net* or call 703-875-2212.

Education is a special focus of the donor community in Khost. An estimated 174,000 students (of whom 40,000 are female) attend schools in the province.

PHOTO BY GRANT HALE

Chapter 1
Overview and Orientation

Khost is a significant province due to its geographic location along the porous border with Pakistan. Khost is an important part of the transit route between Kabul and Pakistan, through which illicit trade and insurgents often pass. Khost has therefore been the scene of a great deal of violence and insurgent activity.

Khostis have seen many changes of power in their lifetimes. During the Communist rule, a large number of well-educated people formed into a ruling class to win influence over and suppress the uneducated rural residents. After the communists were overthrown, Khost welcomed the Taliban, whose tight control and strict decrees quickly soured their support in the province. Today, both the Haqqani Network and Hezb-e Islami Gulbuddin (HIG) are active in the province.

These constant upheavals have taught Khostis that the best survival method is to hedge their bets. The majority remains neutral in the hopes that they can weather any outcome, though economic needs may push some to cooperate with insurgents when other opportunities are unavailable.

ORIENTATION

Lying in southeast Afghanistan, Khost is about the size of Rhode Island, covering 4,235 sq km. Estimates of the provincial population vary widely and no reliable estimates exist of population by district. For the 2005 parliamentary elections, the Central Statistics Office estimated the population to be 478,000. However, in 2006, the Khost Directorate of Census and Population increased this estimate to 1.3 million.

Khost was originally a district within the large province of Loya Paktya which consisted of modern day Paktya, Paktika, and Khost. However, in 1990 Khost became a separate province. Modern day Khost borders the Afghan provinces of Paktya to the north and west, and Paktika to the southwest. It shares a 185 km border with the Pakistan tribal areas of North Waziristan and Kurram Agency – parts of Pakistan's conflicted Federally Administered Tribal Areas (FATA). Trade routes stretching from Karachi to Kabul cut across the province making their way through the cosmopolitan Khost City at its center. The porous border has not only created opportunity for smuggling and illicit activity, but has made Khost a flashpoint of fighting between insurgents and Afghan government and coalition forces.

The Khost Valley and the surrounding mountains dominate the province. Limited rangelands run north to south, bound by forests on the north, south, and west. Khost summers are hot, with temperatures reaching 122 degrees Fahrenheit in the summer. Although poorly irrigated, the Khost Valley is fertile and produces walnuts, fruits, wheat, rice, and corn. Many Khostis keep bees and harvest their honey for the marketplace. Barley is commonly grown in the mountainous area. Most people raise chickens, goats, cows, or sheep for food.

Districts

The province is composed of 12 districts, plus the capital area "Khost (Matun)," which has no district government. Khost City dominates this area, and the mayor of Khost City is the de facto head of the government for Matun. However, the mayor has no formal authority over the other two sections of Matun: Lakan to the east of the city, and Shamal to the southeast (not to be confused with the Shamal district in the west.)

Each district has a center, with a compound for the district sub-governor, his staff, and other key district offices, usually including the Directorates of Education, Health, Agriculture, Rural Rehabilitation and Development, and Mustafiat (Finance). Police and often the National Directorate of Security (NDS) are also present in districts. They either share the government compound or have their own.

In general, districts along the 185 km border with Pakistan suffer the most violence from anti-government forces. The districts include: Zazi Maidan, Bak, Spera, Gurbuz, Tanai, Terezai, and Khost (Matun). However, fighting is also endemic in the non-border district of Sabari, where the Sabari tribe has a history of rebellion regardless of who is in control.

Mando Zai, Zazi Maidan, and Khost (Matun) are the most developed areas, while Gurbuz, Shamal, Tanai, Qalandar, Spera, and Musa Khel districts are among the least developed. These last three districts are mountainous, sparsely populated, and have few roads, making them hard to access.

Key towns

Khost has one city and a few important towns which are focal points for trade and services. In addition to markets where rural populations can buy and sell goods, higher levels of health care and education can be found in these population centers and in the surrounding areas.

Khost City is the hub of government, services, higher education, and business for the province. It attracts students and laborers from all districts, as well as neighboring Pakistan. It provides goods and services that cannot be found elsewhere in the province. For example, it is the only place in Khost where there is any selection of cars to buy – most of them used.

There has been a frenzy of building in Khost City. Thanks to projects such as a new 38-acre provincial government complex being constructed by the Khost Provincial Reconstruction Team (PRT) through the Commander's Emergency Response Program (CERP), most government directorates are getting new offices.

Kholbesat in Sabari district is the largest town outside Khost City, with 300 families and 700 shops. While not the district capital, it is an important center of trade. Nevertheless, the road from Khost City is very dangerous due to the dedicated minority of people here who assist insurgents.

Ali Sher is a small bazaar town and an important center for the eastern Terezai district (aka Ali Sher). Lying northeast of Khost City along a 20 km stretch of paved roads, the area is quiet but tense, as insurgents usually travel through the area, but do not stay for long.

The Shamal (aka Dwamonda) district center, **Dwamonda,** lies in the midst of mountains on the Khost-Gardez road near the border with Paktya, about 30 km from Khost City. It has one fairly conservative madrassa, a large mosque, and a high school that enrolls about 10 percent of youth of appropriate age in the surrounding area. As laws against deforestation are rarely enforced, Dwamonda has become an important supplier of illegally harvested firewood to other districts in Khost, as well as Kabul. Returns from the illicit timber trade are used to recruit fighters to act against the government.

The road from Khost to Dwamonda is currently being repaired. Work on the road is conducted seasonally: during the summer, work is conducted on the Paktya side; during the winter, work is done on the Khost side. The road was scheduled to be completed in 2009 however the project has run into several delays and, at the time of publication, is behind schedule.

Dwamonda is also known as a center of power for the mujahedin leader Jalaludin Haqqani, making it an area unfriendly to the coalition. In November 2008, the Haqqani Network destroyed the district government center with a vehicle borne improvised explosive device (VBIED). A new location across the Dwamonda River is under consideration.

Although only 30 km from Khost City, construction work on the road connecting **Zazi Maidan Town** and the provincial capital has been abandoned due to insecurity in neighboring Sabari and Bak districts. Meanwhile, Zazi Maidan is well connected to Pakistan via a paved road. Surprisingly, the area is relatively quiet and friendly to the coalition.

A new district government center is under construction on a hill above Zazi Maidan. Using CERP funds, the PRT is building a Center of Education Excellence, where secular and religious subjects will be taught.

Dragai, the Tanai district center, is about 10 km southwest of Khost City and can be accessed easily by paved roads. Connected to Gurbuz district by a new gravel road funded by the US Agency for International Development (USAID), Dragai houses a primary school for girls' and boys' education facilities up to high school level, and a basic health clinic. The area around Dragai sees little insurgent activity, but crime (such as kidnapping) remains a traditional way for the tribes to earn money.

Map 1. Population Map of Khost

Legend:
- Roads
- District Border
- River
- Provincial Center
- City

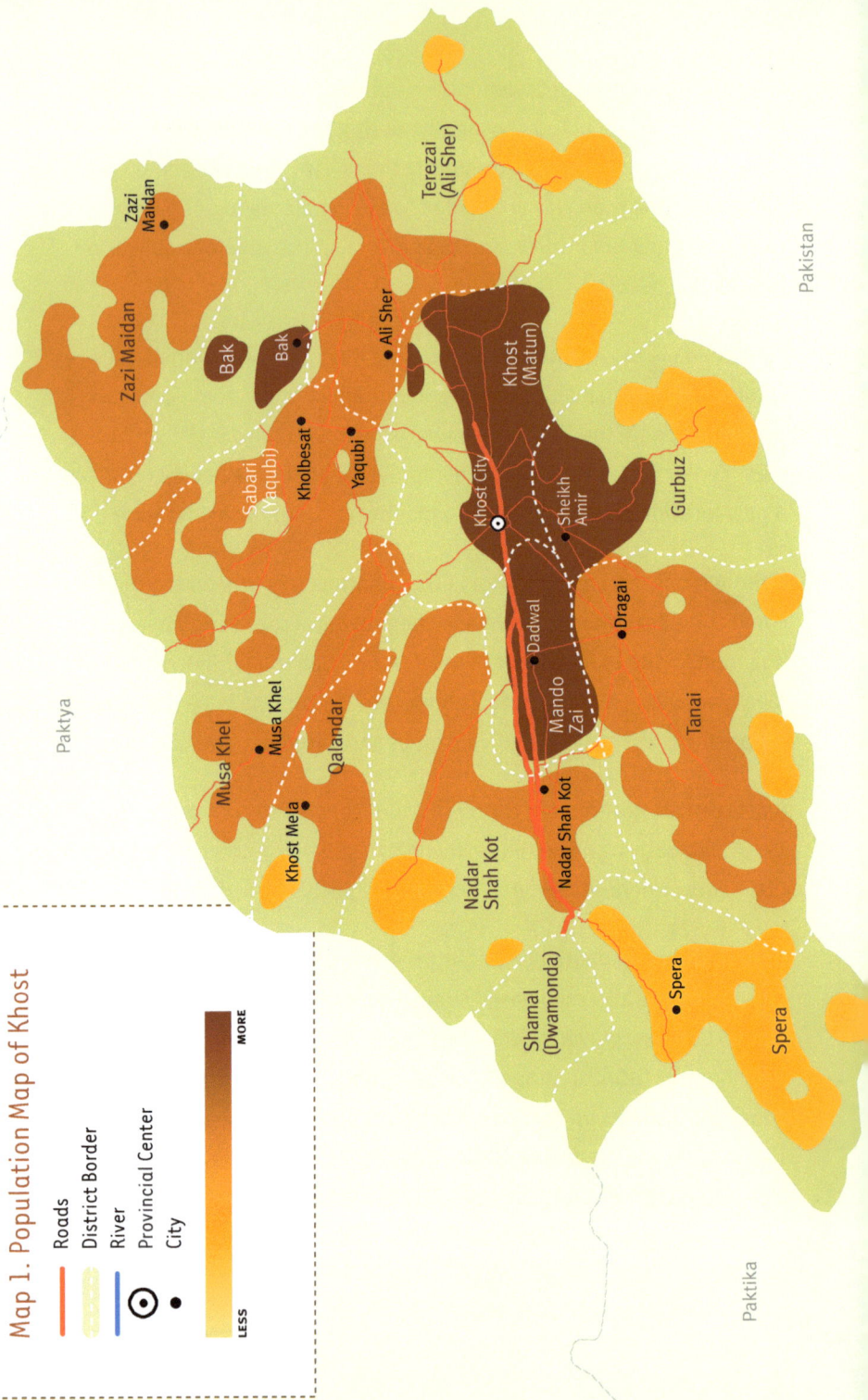

LESS — MORE

Labels:
Zazi Maidan
Zazi Maidan (city)
Terezai (Ali Sher)
Pakistan
Bak
Bak
Ali Sher
Ali Sher
Khost (Matun)
Sabari (Yaqubi)
Kholbesat
Yaqubi
Khost City
Sheikh Amir
Gurbuz
Musa Khel
Musa Khel
Qalandar
Dadwal
Dragai
Tanai
Mando Zai
Khost Mela
Nadar Shah Kot
Nadar Shah Kot
Spera
Spera
Shamal (Dwamonda)
Spera
Paktya
Paktika

Table 1: District Populations

DISTRICT	DISTRICT CENTER	EST. POP. FROM CSO 2006	MAJOR PASHTUN TRIBES
Bak	Bak	51,160	Babaker Khel, Ali Sher, Terazai
Gurbuz	Sheikh Amir	60,560	Gurbuz, Kuchi, Waziri
Zazi Maidan	Zazi Maidan	55,870	Zazi
Khost (Matun)	Khost City	316,900	Mix of all tribes
Mando Zai (Ismael Khel)	Dadwal	130,520	Mando Zai, Ismail Khel, Zadran, Mangal
Musa Khel	Musa Khel	94,760	Mangal
Nadar Shah Kot	Nadar Shah Kot	73,880	Zadran, Mangal
Qalandar	Khost Mela	23,760	Zadran, Mangal
Sabari (Yaqubi)	Yaqubi	163,970	Sabari, Mangal
Shamal (Dwamonda)	Dwamonda	31,330	Zadran
Spera	Spera	56,130	Zadran, Kharoti, Sulimankhel
Tanai	Dragai	137,840	Tanai, Pieran
Terezai (Ali Sher)	Ali Sher	103,380	Terazai, Ali Sher, Mangal, Zadran
TOTAL		1,300,060	

RELEVANT HISTORICAL ISSUES

From Ancient to Modern Times

During the 19th century wars with the British, Loya Paktya changed
hands several times. When the issue was finally settled, the Durand
Line (which delineated Pakistan from Afghanistan) cut through tribes
from within Loya Paktya, putting some tribes and family members in
Pakistan and some in Afghanistan. This disputed border was drawn
in 1893 by the British and signed by the Afghan king under duress.
Pashtuns claim the border was to expire in 100 years, but there is
nothing in the treaty or the historical record on that point. The line
divides many tribes of Khost, such as the Gurbuz. These divided
families ascribe no significance to the border to this day.

In 1929, the Mangal tribe of Loya Paktya (of which Khost was then
part) helped Mohammad Nadir Shah overthrow the Tajik king of
Afghanistan, Habibullah Kalakani, thus returning the monarchy to
Pashtun hands. In recognition of their contribution, the king granted
the people of Loya Paktya an exemption from state taxes and military
conscription, and promised them minimal state intervention and
the right to bear arms. Despite the king's assassination four years
later, this agreement was upheld until the central government began
building roads and schools in the province in the 1950s. This sudden
involvement by the national government sparked a tribal revolt led by
the Mangal tribe. The government quickly withdrew and accepted the
status quo.

Communist Era (1979-1992)

After Kabul, Khost was the strongest center of power for the Communist Party in Afghanistan. The Communists targeted the province for tight control due to its strategic location on the eastern border and the relatively high number of educated people who could work for the government. Several Khostis held government positions at the national level, making Khost an influential province in national politics.

Thousands of Afghan volunteers, many from Khost, joined the jihad against the Soviets. Each round of conflict prompted a wave of emigrations to Pakistan. These refugees became recruits for the mujahedin, thus perpetuating the conflict.

Hezb-e Islami Gulbuddin (HIG) and several other smaller groups operated in the Khost area, where they received support from the US Government through Pakistan's Inter-Services Intelligence (ISI). Jalaludin Haqqani was the most prominent commander in the Khost area, keeping his base in Miram Shah, Pakistan. The mujahedin strategy sought to re-occupy Khost and control the Khost-Gardez pass in an attempt to cut off the Soviet supply lines from Kabul.

Mujahedin and Taliban (1992-2001)

Following the Soviet withdrawal, the Communist government attempted to reconcile with mujahedin forces and keep power. In the process, mujahedin commander Jalaludin Haqqani took control of the province and Khost became the first area to slip from government control. There was no reconciliation, and the Communists were overthrown.

Mujahedin factions soon began to fight among themselves, and Khost became lawless. People fled the deteriorating cities and lived off what they could grow in the country or procure from Pakistan. A series of attempts to unite the warring factions and stabilize the area was unsuccessful.

In 1996, Haqqani and other powerful commanders joined the Taliban after they took control of Kabul. This union enabled the Taliban to take tighter control of Khost than most other areas. Indeed, Osama bin Laden likely chose this area for his al-Qaeda training camp due to Khost's strong Taliban influence and proximity to Pakistan.

Though most conservative rural people felt affinity for the Taliban's focus on religion, the severe restrictions imposed by the Taliban quickly made Khostis unhappy. For instance, the women of Khost were used to working in the fields while daughters went to the mosques to study. The Taliban strictly curtailed women's movements in public, a policy which the public did not support. Similarly, people grew weary of unabated poverty, which the Taliban could not effectively address.

In one stark example of Taliban rule, the family of a murdered Pakistani demanded punishment of the Afghan who had killed him. The Taliban arrested the killer and allowed the victim's family to execute him in public. The manner in which the Taliban carried out the death sentence triggered a nationalistic backlash. Even today, people refer to this incident as a source of anti-Pakistani feelings.

Contemporary Events (2002-present)

During the US-led invasion of Afghanistan, the Taliban and their mujahedin supporters fought the militias of brothers Pacha Khan Zadran and Kamal Khan Zadran. The older brother and primary commander, Pacha, took control of Paktya, while Kamal led forces in Khost.

The brothers held the region until 2002, when the central government took control of the province and appointed a new governor, Hakim Tanaiwal. All governors since have been tightly linked to Kabul. They have had varied amounts of success based on their managerial skills and the availability of funds for reconstruction and development. Pacha Khan is now a Member of Parliament (MP) from Paktya, while Kamal's whereabouts are unknown.

In 2006, the US, the provincial government of Khost, and Afghanistan National Security Forces (ANSF) jointly decided to station US forces in district government centers. The intent was to co-locate US forces with ANSF in order to train them and demonstrate security. However, the teams became targets for attacks. In summer 2008, two suicide bombers attacked the Gurbuz district center followed by a series of VBIED attacks whose targets included Shamal and Mando Zai district centers. To avoid further attacks on district centers, coalition forces are relocating to separate bases nearby.

Khost remains a strategic border province coveted by anti-government forces. Insecurity remains the primary limiting factor on progress. It has restricted the government's National Solidarity Program to half the districts *(see Ch. 5)*. Corruption has increased the costs of foreign-funded infrastructure because many officials are taking money from projects.

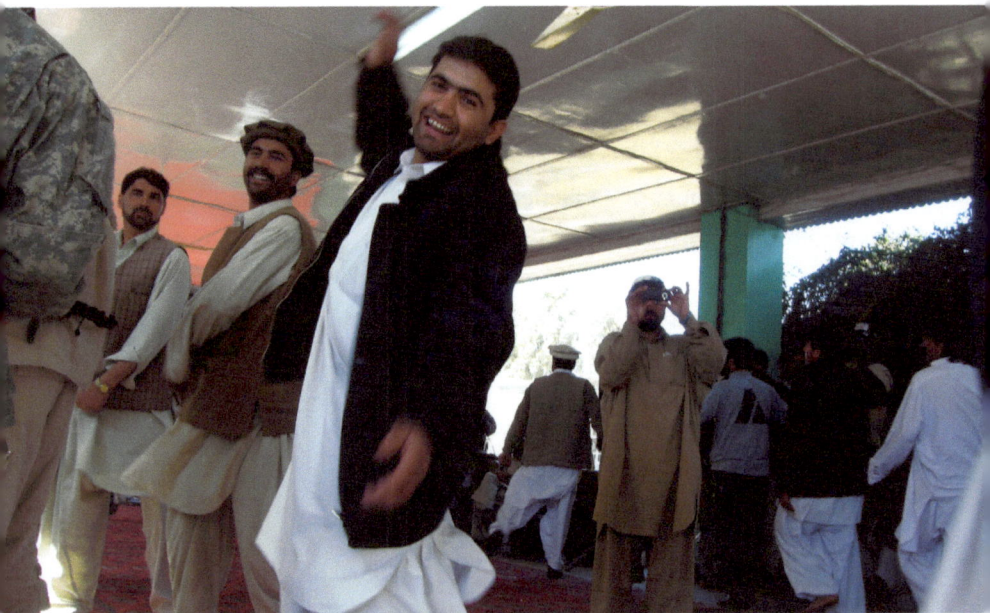

Men perform atan, *a traditional Afghan dance. Numerous aspects of Khosti life, from the* attan *to the Pashtunwali code, are centuries-old institutions.*

PHOTO BY GRANT HALE

Chapter 2
Ethnicity, Tribes,
Language, and Religion

ETHNICITY

Khost's population is 99 percent Pashtun. The terms "Khostwal" or "Khosti" are often mistakenly used to describe the tribes of Khost, however these terms merely refer to anyone from Khost irrespective of tribe. While tribal heritage is important in understanding a Khosti's disposition, other factors also shape attitudes. For example, better-educated people in Khost City are usually more open-minded than their rural tribal affiliates.

TRIBES

Next to the family unit, the tribe remains the most important system of social organization within Pashtun society. Decision-making is conducted by elders and eminent persons through two primary mechanisms.

The first is a *jirga*, a meeting held to make a specific decision. A decision made in a jirga is supposedly binding, but this relies on the strength of complicated social networks, which are not nearly as strong as they were 30 years ago.

Table 2: Major Tribes in Khost

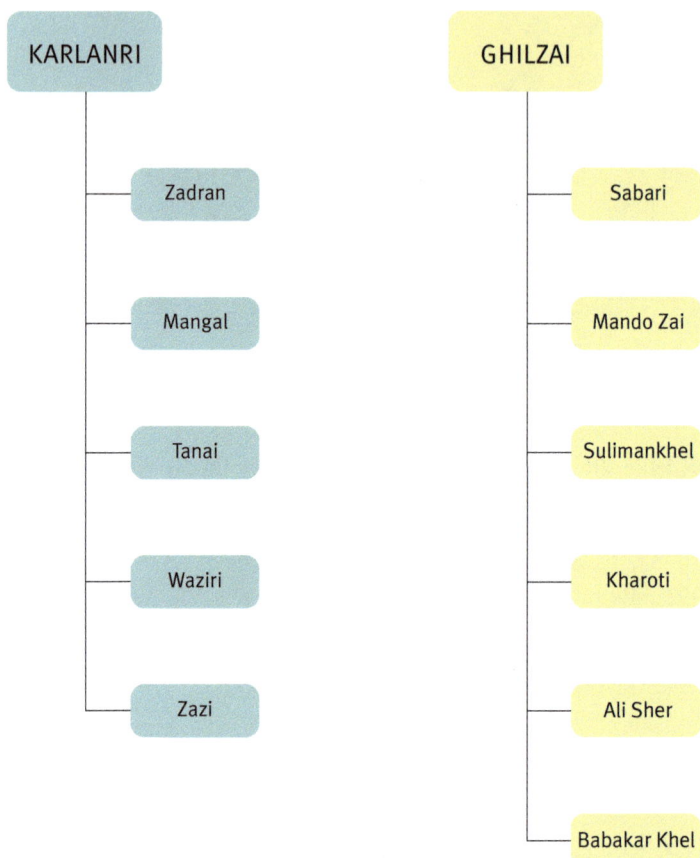

KARLANRI
- Zadran
- Mangal
- Tanai
- Waziri
- Zazi

GHILZAI
- Sabari
- Mando Zai
- Sulimankhel
- Kharoti
- Ali Sher
- Babakar Khel

The other mechanism is a *shura*, from the Arabic word for consultation. Shuras are usually standing bodies that can be called together to do things such as redress wrongs through arbitration, or act as an advisory council on a community's issues.

Tribal leaders resolve disputes and have an important role in maintaining law and order. In many places, police are under-resourced, so arbakai militias led by tribal leaders fill the vacuum. Every tribe maintains arbakai for their local interests *(please see Chapter 3 for a full description of arbakai)*.

Pashtunwali

Society in Khost is structured around *pashtunwali*, "the way of the Pashtuns," a pre-Islamic code of conduct. All Pashtuns have some knowledge of the code and will try to follow it. Some tribes are stricter than others. The four main parts of pashtunwali are as follows:

Nang (Honor): All Pashtuns are required to uphold the honor of their family and their tribe by following the code. An insult to someone's tribe or family can lead to revenge. The biggest disputes are over women, land, and money; a Pashtun man must protect these three with his life and honor.

Melmastia (Hospitality): Pashtuns are known for their hospitality, and will go to great lengths to treat their guests with honor and respect. Most villages and large families will have a dedicated guesthouse. Even if a family has limited resources, a stranger will still be welcomed, fed, and given a place to sleep. Coalition personnel will often be offered more hospitality than they can accept. It is advisable to accept as much hospitality as possible, and to refuse further hospitality gracefully.

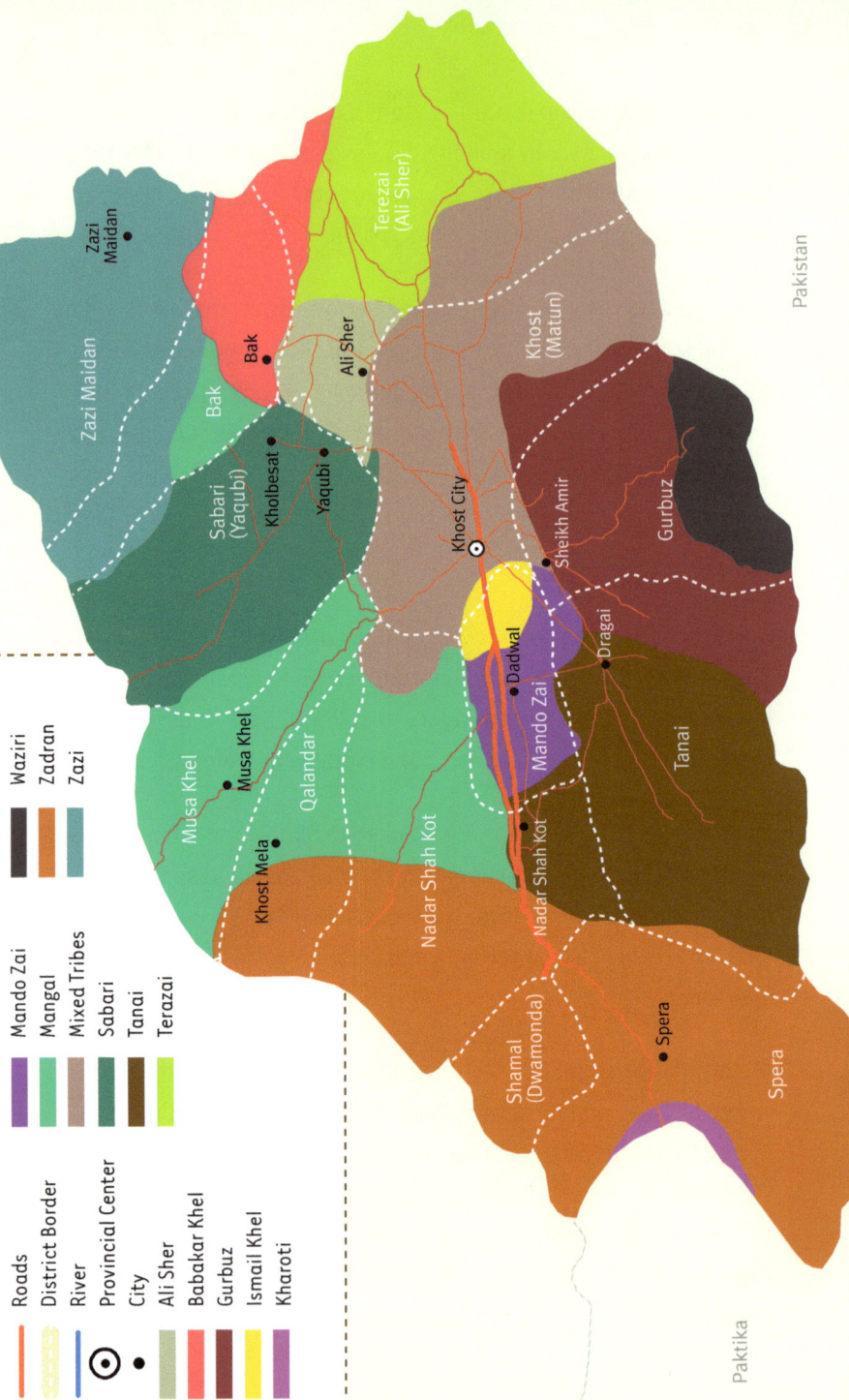

Map 2. Tribal Map of Khost

Legend:

Roads
District Border
River
Provincial Center
City

Ali Sher
Babakar Khel
Gurbuz
Ismail Khel
Kharoti

Mando Zai
Mangal
Mixed Tribes
Sabari
Tanai
Terazai

Waziri
Zadran
Zazi

Regions labeled on map:

Zazi Maidan
Zazi Maidan
Bak
Bak
Terezai (Ali Sher)
Ali Sher
Khost (Matun)
Sabari (Yaqubi)
Kholbesat
Yaqubi
Khost City
Sheikh Amir
Gurbuz
Musa Khel
Musa Khel
Qalandar
Dadwal
Mando Zai
Dragai
Tanai
Khost Mela
Nadar Shah Kot
Nadar Shah Kot
Shamal (Dwamonda)
Spera
Spera

Pakistan

Paktika

Nanawatay (Sanctuary): Anyone who commits a minor crime can admit guilt and ask forgiveness. A jirga will hear the complaint and may propose payment in cash or livestock. Upon completion of payment, the injured party forgives the crime. Often women will arrange for this, as they are considered natural peacemakers. Nanawatay can also be used to beg for mercy and protection, but it does not apply to major or repeated crimes. Payments by foreign military after accidental deaths, e.g. through solatia, can fall within Nanawatay.

Badal (Revenge): Pashtuns will take revenge for an insult or crime, even if it takes decades. It is the only way to restore honor. A current conflict may have its roots generations back. Perceived injustices by foreigners may lose the friendship of an entire clan for generations.

Prominent Tribes of Khost

Tribes in Khost are numerous and complex. The Karlanri and Ghilzai "super tribes" make up the majority of Pashtuns in Khost. The Karlanri, Durrani, and Ghilzai Pashtuns often see each other as rivals – a relationship that has played out on the national stage and in the civil war. The Taliban have historically drawn most of their supporters from Ghilzai. Today many Ghilzai perceive the Durrani and Karlanri as oppressors with a grip on power. Nevertheless, there is some dispute regarding the extent to which tribal affiliations can be used as an indicator of an individual's disposition towards the Afghan government and coalition forces. Loyalties can and do shift often in Afghanistan. Below are descriptions of a few of the most significant tribes listed in descending order according to population.

The largest tribe in all of Loya Paktya (Khost, Paktya, and Paktika), the **Zadran** is a Karlanri tribe and in Khost resides predominantly in Spera. The most influential member is Jalaludin Haqqani, an anti-government leader from Paktya. Due to his influence, Zadran tribesmen are often opposed to the central government and coalition forces and give refuge to Taliban fighters. The Zadran controls the territory around the Khost-Gardez road. If the Taliban begin a campaign against this route, the cooperation of the Zadran will be critical to keeping this main thoroughfare secure.

The **Mangal**, a Karlanri tribe, is located primarily in Qalander and Musa Khel. It had had a history of rebelling against local governors and appointees of the central government. However, it now supports the central government and coalition forces.

The **Tanai** tribe is Karlanri and lives primarily in Tanai district. In general, tribesmen are reliable supporters of the central government, although criminals from Tanai have recently committed kidnapping, car-jacking, and armed robbery. These criminals are usually motivated by economics rather than politics.

The **Waziri** tribe is Karlanri and lives primarily in Gurbuz and Nadar Shah Kot. Historically most members have supported whoever was in charge of the government. Though the Waziri in Khost originally came from Waziristan in the FATA region of Pakistan, many no longer have close ties to their distant relatives there.

The **Sabari** is a Ghilzai tribe which lives in Sabari district. The tribe has a history of rebelling against the government, regardless of who was in control, and this continues today. The Sabari is known as the most conservative tribe in Khost and the district sees extensive fighting. Sabari district is home to more than half of all IEDs placed in Khost. The current acting governor of Khost is from Sabari.

The **Zazi** is a Karlanri tribe living in Zazi Maidan district. They are a rural, poor, and remote people, yet they are more open-minded than many rural tribes; for example, they support girls' education. Historically, they have been peaceful, supporting local and national governments.

In Khost, the **Sulimankhel** reside in Spera. It is the largest tribe in Paktika and remains a source of recruits for the Taliban.

The **Kharoti**, a Ghilzai tribe, is located in Spera district. Its most famous member is Gulbuddin Hekmatyar, leader of Hezb-e Islami Gulbuddin (HIG), a major insurgent group in Afghanistan.

Kuchis are Pashtun nomads, but are not a tribe; about 30,000 live in Khost. Some have settled in Khost (Matun) and Bak. The remainder lives in Khost in the cool season, and moves to higher rangelands of neighboring provinces in the warm months.

Tribal Conflicts

Current inter-tribal antagonisms are minor. Government structures and the international community have been successful in resolving many tribal disputes in recent years. For example, in 2006 the Attorney General and UNAMA brokered an agreement in a long-running land dispute between the Babakar Khel and Mangal.

LANGUAGE

Most Khostis speak Pashto, with each tribe having its own distinct dialect. A few people who have migrated from northern Afghanistan to Khost City speak Dari, but all learn Pashto quickly.

The extended family is the basic unit of social organization. In rural families, female members work largely in the dwelling while male members might work in the fields, earn a wage outside the home, or even send remittances back from a job abroad.

PHOTO BY: GRANT HALE

ROLE OF RELIGION

Islam plays an important part in the lives of Khostis, most of whom are conservative Sunni Muslims, especially in the rural areas. Most pray five times a day and go to mosques. Almost everyone makes a show of piety, regardless of belief. The majority of Khost men grow beards. Men cover their head with turbans, pakols, or prayer caps. Women wear brightly colored burqas in public. The basis for the manner of dress is a combination of religion and Pashtun culture, which people may not separate.

No outsider should talk poorly about Islam or accuse an Afghan of being un-Islamic. It is good to compliment someone for being a good Muslim, but the topic of religion should be approached lightly, if at all. Since the Koran is seen by Muslims as an infallible document, delivered to the Prophet directly by God, any debate on particulars of Islamic belief and practice should not be entered into.

THE FAMILY UNIT

The family is the primary unit of social organization, usually comprising 10-100 people at home. Male members earn income, while women and older members stay home. When there is high unemployment and the family cannot subsist on its land, this system breaks down, driving the young to migrate.

Khost's strong extended families are often supported by a male member working abroad. A majority of Khostis working abroad are in the UAE. Their families survive on, and many prosper from, remittances that they send home from abroad.

Afghans gather for a tribal shura. Shuras are one of informal systems of governance used by community leaders to make decisions. They are focused more on redressing wrongs through arbitration or addressing issues of pride than exacting punishment. All members of the shura must agree before a decision is made.

PHOTO BY RAHMATULLAH KAWSAR

Chapter 3
Government and Leadership

HOW THE GOVERNMENT OFFICIALLY WORKS

Central Control

Authority and power in Afghanistan are concentrated in the national government as a means to counter the power of warlords in the provinces. As such, the provincial government is limited to an advisory role for the central government, while decisions on everything from policy to funding priorities are made in Kabul.

Provincial Government

A governor (*wali*) heads the provincial government and reports to the Independent Directorate for Local Governance (IDLG) located in the Executive Office of the President.

Ministries in Kabul appoint provincial directors (with presidential approval) to execute their policies and programs. The director reports to and receives funds from the ministry in Kabul, with the governor outside the chain of command. However, the governor must approve all expenditures by the directorates in the province before they are processed by the Director of Finance (*Mustafiat*).

The Provincial Council (PC), the only elected body at the provincial level, advises on provincial issues. The PC reports directly to the president but has no budget. Its relevance is largely dependent on the governor's support and on its members' individual resources and initiatives. In 2007, the Provincial Council gained authority to approve the Provincial Development Plan (PDP), allowing PC members some ability to represent their constituents. Each province has completed a PDP, linked to the Afghan National Development Strategy (ANDS), laying out its goals for provincial development.

The Provincial Development Committee (PDC) is responsible for developing and overseeing the implementation of the PDP. The PDC is composed of provincial representatives of the ministries (otherwise referred to as line directors) and is chaired by the governor, with the Director of Economy serving as the Secretariat. The governor can invite PC members, elders, and members of the international community and NGOs as non-voting members to ensure coordination among development actors. Participants often include: the PRT (both the military and USAID), NGOs, and the UN. Technical Working Groups (TWGs) are established by sector (in accordance with the ANDS) and report their findings/recommendations to the PDC.

District and Local Governance

Government at the district level mirrors the provincial government with the *woluswal* (district sub-governor), district police chief, and NDS officer. Some ministries have representatives at the district level, but not in every district. In 2007, District Development Assemblies (DDA) were formed in order to plan, prioritize, and coordinate development activities at the district level and to feed local input into the PDP.

Recently, several provinces have begun establishing district shuras under the Afghan Social Outreach Program (ASOP), a program overseen by IDLG and funded by the US and UK, among others. It seeks to empower local communities to engage with development issues, build social capital, channel the grievances of the people and assume greater responsibility for local-level security. Under ASOP, council members would be paid 6,000 Afs ($120) a month. The program has become controversial, as critics claim it is an attempt by the central government to buy the loyalty of local leaders. The selection process of district shura members is still unclear.

Below the district level, the only formal governance structures are Community Development Councils (CDCs) established by the National Solidarity Program (NSP). CDCs do not have an established role in Afghan law.

The municipality of Khost is run by a mayor appointed by IDLG in consultation with the governor. Municipalities are independent from the provincial government, are free to plan, fund, and implement projects, and are the only entities the provincial level that can levy taxes. There is often only one municipality in a province, usually the capital and largest population center.

HOW IT ACTUALLY WORKS

The governor has undisputed authority within the Khost provincial government, even though he does not have formal jurisdiction over the representatives of the ministries. A January 2009 law passed by the Afghan Parliament gives the governor formal control over ANP in the province. It also gives district sub-governors control over ANP at the district level. The governor and sub-governors also have the closest relationship with the PRT and other donors, and they keep support among the citizens through their ability to influence donor-funded projects.

The primary alternate source of power in the province comes from force and fear. The Haqqani Network and those that harbor it in the border areas and other districts, such as Sabari, compete with the formal government for the loyalty of the populace. Tribal elders have strong influence over small areas, but they are often overshadowed by warlords and insurgents.

The Khost municipal and provincial governments provide services and have strong influence in the provincial center. However, in most districts, the local tribal leaders are the main authorities. The formal government is ineffective in most districts, where officials do not perform well. For example, crimes in the center often bring investigation, capture, and punishment of the offender, but most people believe that even a murder in the rural districts is beyond the reach of the criminal justice system.

POLITICAL PARTIES

Most political parties in Afghanistan are little more than cliques formed around a charismatic personality or to promote a specific interpretation of Islam. Hence they tend not to play a significant role in the political process. Some of the more active in Khost are listed in Table 2.

SECURITY FORCES

Among the main official security actors in the province are the Afghan National Police (ANP), Afghan National Army (ANA), and the National Directorate for Security (NDS). Coordination Centers have been established by the US military and provide a location where coalition and Afghan forces can work together to monitor problems in real time. A Joint Provincial Coordination Center (JPCC) is located near the governor's compound, and Joint District Coordination Centers (JDCCs) are located in some district capitals.

Table 3: Major Political Parties

PARTY NAME	NOTES
Hezb-e Islami Khalis (HIK)	Originally a mujahideen group which broke away from HIG under the leadership of Yunus Khalis. When Khalis died in 2006, the party became active in the legitimate political process.
Hezb-e Afghan Millat (Afghan Nation Party)	An ethno-nationalist Pashtun, anti-Tajik party that has grown in popularity as more people believe that Karzai has given too much authority to former Northern Alliance mujahedin. Led by Mohammed Rahim.
Mahaz-e Milli Islami (National Islamic Front)	A party started and led by Pir Ishaq Gailani. It promotes national unity and is influential among certain Sufis; former Governor Hamidullah Qalandarzai was a member.
Hezb-e Afghanistan Naween (New Afghanistan Party)	Part of a larger political alliance called the National Understanding Front.
Hezb-e Islami Afghanistan (HIA)	Although sometimes still referred to as HIG (Hezb-e Islami Gulbuddin), this is the peaceful offshoot of that anti-government group. It claims to have 30 members in Parliament, though not all former members of the HIG militia openly announce their membership.
Jamiat-e Islami	A Tajik political movement.

Afghan National Army (ANA)

The ANA is perhaps the most functional Afghan security institution. By late 2008, the ANA had surpassed 80,000 soldiers, with plans to reach 140,000. The ANA tries to maintain ethnic balance, but Tajiks and Pashtuns are over-represented in the officer class, and Hazaras and other minorities are significantly under-represented. Pashtuns in the army tend to come from eastern provinces such as Khost, not from the south. The ANA suffers from a chronic lack of educated leaders and bureaucrats.

Brigadier General Mohammad Israr Aqdas is the commander of 1st Brigade, 203rd Corps in Khost. It maintains security through coopera- tion with the ANP (and the Afghan National Border Police as part of the ANP), NDS, and coalition forces. In May 2009, all five of the brigade's kandaks (battalions) achieved the highest readiness rating, Capability Milestone 1, the first brigade in the entire ANA to do so. People in Khost are generally happy with the performance of ANA. They are thought to be more professional and better equipped than Afghan Uniformed Police (AUP) and ANBP, and have been gradually improving under the mentorship of the US Army trainers. In joint Afghan-coalition opera- tions, more than 50 percent of the soldiers are Afghan. On average an ANA soldier makes 10,000 Afs per month (about $200).

Afghan National Police (ANP)

The Afghan National Police have acquired an extremely poor reputation in many parts of the country. In Khost, they appear to have a slightly better reputation, but they are still considered corrupt. Because the ANP are generally paid less than the ANA, they tend to get lower quality candidates. They have a reputation for routine bribery, extortion, criminality, and incompetence. Narcotics abuse is a problem in many police units.

Table 4: Provincial Security Officials

NAME	POSITION	ORGANIZATION	MOBILE NUMBER
Mohammad Yaqub Mandozai	Acting Provincial Chief of Police	ANP	0799-315-569
Brigadier General Mohammad Israr Aqdas	Commander	1st Brigade, 203rd Corps, ANA	0799-033-628
Nabi Jan Mullahkhail	Chief of Police	ANBP	N/A
General Abdul Momin	Head	NDS	0799-033-628
Saranwal Roshan	Prosecutor	Prosecutor	0700-078-040
Nowroz Ousoli	Head	State Judiciary Office	0799-149-020

Source(s): UNAMA SER Political Section, September 2008

Basic police training lasts 10 weeks and takes place at regional training centers. About 40 police are deployed to each district. They are poorly equipped and paid about 500-10,000 Afs ($100-200) per month through direct deposit, depending on rank. While above average for Afghan civil servants, pay is often late. Police are vulnerable to Taliban attacks. In 2007, the Taliban killed 900 police officers nationwide, often in attacks on poorly manned checkpoints in remote areas.

The ANP are active in Khost (Matun) and are viewed positively there for their effectiveness in maintaining security. Of note, they are credited with catching suicide bombers at checkpoints at the edges of Khost City.

The ANP are not viewed positively in the rest of the province. When US troops were co-located with ANP in district centers, the ANP were forced to get out and patrol the local areas on foot. However, as the US moves to nearby but separate locations, the ANP are no longer as active on its own.

Afghan National Border Police (ANBP)

The ANBP is administered by the Ministry of Interior and maintains security at the borders. In Khost, it is commanded by Nabi Jan Mullahkhail. Because the border with Pakistan is such a dangerous area, the ANBP has a hard time recruiting and keeping police. However, despite frequent attacks, the ANBP has not abandoned any checkpoints. With renewed US interest in the Afghanistan-Pakistan border region, it is expected that staffing, training, equipment, and salaries will improve.

National Directorate of Security (NDS)

The National Directorate of Security is Afghanistan's domestic security agency. Many of its members are former communist-era government officials and Pashtuns often claim that it is dominated by Tajiks. The NDS has faced criticism from international human rights groups and Western media organizations for alleged torture of suspects. Nevertheless, it is thought to have some good human intelligence networks, but relies on Western technological assistance for electronic intelligence gathering.

The NDS in Khost is led by General Momin, who is viewed favorably by most Khostis. It is credited with catching suicide bombers and has been targeted by anti-government forces, including a large VBIED attack on their provincial complex in early December 2008.

Arbakai

In addition to official security forces, Khost and nearby provinces have a tradition of tribal militias known as arbakai. This centuries-old institution developed as a community policing mechanism made up of volunteers who follow a strict ethical code. Each group of arbakai receives orders from tribal leaders. The arbakai maintain security and in some cases enforce traditional laws. Normally there are 50-60 men per arbakai in each village, but this could be increased up to 300 in extraordinary circumstances. The governments of Afghanistan and the US continue to debate whether to work with the arbakai as separate from the ANSF, through programs such as the Afghan Public Protection Program (AP3), or whether to incorporate the militia members into the national forces.

Table 5: Members of the Provincial Government

NAME	JOB TITLE	CELL PHONE
Tahir Khan Sabari	Acting Governor	0799-288-925
Abdul Ghayas Jalatzai	Director of Environmental Protection Agency	0799-134-220
Taj Ali Sabir	Chair of Provincial Council	0799-135-355
Mir Zaman Narai	Director of Labor, Social Affairs, Martyrs, and the Disabled	0700-782-400 0799-114-592
Haji Qasim Tanai	Director of the Afghan Red Crescent Society	0799-144-748
Said Aziz Ahmad Hashimi	Director of Education	0799-479-456
Hameed Shah	Director of Economy	0799-155-542
Mohmmad Omar Arin	Director of Rural Rehabilitation and Development	0799-046-064
Noor Badshah	Director of Public Health	0777-046-064
Zahir Gul	Director of Agriculture, Irrigation, and Livestock	0799-421-969
Mohammad Shafiq Popal	Director of Information and Culture	0700-161-982 0799-810-969
Bismillah Gul	Director of Refugees	0799-301-957
Awal Khan kohi	Director of Power	0799-010-081
Eng. Eid Markhan	Director of Water (Irrigation)	0799-422-544
Marina Gul Tanaiwal	Director of Counter Narcotics	0799-422-413
Rogul Zadran	Director of Women's Affairs	0799-070-819
Laiq Khan	Director of Mines	0799-136-338
Moamoor Shah	Director of Public Works	0799-134-515

Table 6: District Sub-Governors

DISTRICT	NAME	CONTACT NUMBER
Bak	Said Ahmad Khan Wafa	0799-659-000
Gurbuz	Akbar Zadran	0799-681-876
Zazi Maidan	Yunas Zadran	0799-805-255
Khost City Mayor	N/A	N/A
Mando Zai (Ismael Khel)	Haji Dawlad Khan	0799-135-712
Musa Khel	Mohammad Kamin	0799-443-883 0797-540-593
Nadar Shah Kot	Badi Zaman Sabari	0799-115-076
Qalandar	Abdul Hanan	No cell phone service
Sabari (Yaqubi)	Gul Qasim Jahadyar	0798-163-412
Shamal (Dwamonda)	Lutfullah Babakarkhel	N/A
Spera	Muhammed Azim	0799-556-895 0797-505-253
Tanai	Hakim Noor	N/A
Terezai (Ali Sher)	Mujib Ul Rahman	0799-138-355

LEADER PROFILES

Government Leaders

Former governor **Hamidullah Qalandarzai** was ousted in 2009 following popular accusations of incompetence. Civil society organizations and tribal councils complained about the closure of the Governor's House, criticized the lack of progress on Khost civil airport and the Khost-Gardez Highway, and demanded the reformation of the provincial government and Qalandarzai's resignation. **Deputy Governor Tahir Khan Sabari** has served as Acting Governor since Qalandarzai departed office; as of March 2010, the governorship has not been officially filled.

Table 7: Members of Parliament from Khost

NAME	HOUSE	DISTRICT NAME	VILLAGE NAME	PHONE
Sayed Mohammad Gulabzoy	Wolesi	Nadir Shah Kot	Kapri	0799-425-079
Amir Khan Sabari	Wolesi	Sabari	Maktab	0799-422-676
Layaqatullah Babakarkhel	Wolesi	Bak	Babakar Khel	0799-008-958
Molawi Hanif Shah Husaini	Wolesi	Tanai	Laghuri Peeran	0799-136-992
Sahira Sharif (female)	Wolesi	Khost City	Matun	0799-441-368
Sabir Khan	Meshrano	Bak	Babakar Khel	0799-070-000
Mirbat Mangal	Meshrano	Musal Khel	Laja	0773-374-340

Taj Ali Sabir, PC Chairman: The provincial council is headed by Taj Ali Sabir, of the Sabari tribe. He is reportedly quite popular in his own tribe, but others question his commitment to supporting the government. He had strong influence due to his close ties to former Governor Jamal, though it remains unclear how much influence he will have following Qalandarzai's departure as governor. Saiar studied political science at Nangarhar University and lectured at Khost University in the political science faculty.

Omer Arin, Director of Rural Rehabilitation and Development: RRD receives most of the international funding channeled through the Afghan government, making Arin very influential in Khost. He is considered honest and effective in running several RRD national programs.

Key Non-Government Figures

Jahan Zoi Mangal: An important leader in the business community of Khost, Jahan Zoi Mangal works in the import business, supplying tea, cooking oils, and food to Khost from Pakistan and the UAE.

Ali Akbar Zhowndi: While he does not live in Khost, Zhowndi is a national business leader with many business activities in the province. He has a share in Azizi Bank in Khost and he imports goods from the UAE.

Jalaludin and Sirajuddin Haqqani: Jalaludin Haqqani is a former mujahedin leader who captured Khost from the Communists in 1991. In 1995 he allied himself with the Taliban. Ever since the Taliban were defeated, Haqqani is believed to have been operating out of neighboring Northern Waziristan in Pakistan, from where he organizes attacks against Afghan government and coalition troops in Afghanistan. During the 2009 conflict in Waziristan, Haqqani's forces cooperated with local forces in repelling the Pakistan army. However, Haqqani remains focused mainly on the insurgency in Afghanistan. His son Sirajuddin Haqqani now runs the organization, but both are still active in disruptive operations in Khost. They have connections with al-Qaeda and Inter-Services Intelligence (ISI), Pakistan's intel agency. The Haqqanis are Zadrans from Paktya province. As Jalauluddin Haqqani is the leader of opposition forces he is obliged to agree with the positions taken by the Taliban against the Pakistani authorities. For example, Haqqani and his forces are directly involved in all conflicts in Waziristan because he and his forces are stationed inside Wazirsatan and they have to cooperate with other opposition leaders there. Haqqani's forces are influential in the border areas of Khost as well as Zadran area. His insurgent activities are planned and designed from this area.

Khost enjoys fertile soil and a moderate climate, though inefficient irrigation limits the production of surplus food.

PHOTO BY RAHMATULLAH KAWSAR

Chapter 4
The Economy

Khost's economy has recently boomed. High-rise buildings have sprung up inside Khost City and other districts, such as Mando Zai, Nadar Shah Kot and Zazi Maidan. However, private builders have not used transparent methods to obtain government land in strategic areas.

Khost is fortunate to have growing commercial, transportation, and financial sectors. There are around 11,000 shops in the province, a large number of which are in Khost City. Those within Khost City pay taxes to the Khost municipal government, a total of about 90,000 Afs ($1,800) per month.

The economy in Khost is heavily dominated by trade with Pakistan. Most construction materials, fuel, cooking gas, and medicines are brought in from Pakistan. Likewise, most shops use Pakistani rupees (or khaldars) as their currency of choice, instead of the Afghani.

The Khost customs house collects tariffs on goods that come into the province from Pakistan. The reported monthly income of the Khost customs office averages 33 million Afs ($660,000), which is sent to the Ministry of Finance in Kabul. However, the customs collection system lacks transparency, making it unclear if more money is collected than is reported.

There are three banks operating in Khost. Kabul Bank and Azizi Bank are private, while Da Afghanistan Bank (DAB) is the central government bank. Government salaries are paid electronically from Kabul through DAB sometimes to individual accounts. Banking transactions in the province total 300 million Afs ($6 million) per month. Most local aid organizations, foreign governments, and the military pay contractors through the private banks.

Western Union has offices inside of the private banks in Khost. However, with the large number of Khostwals working abroad, money exchangers now offer services transferring payments to and from other countries.

INFRASTRUCTURE

Electricity

The Ministry of Energy and Water operates five generators in Khost City. Of these, three were provided by the Khost PRT through CERP. They can generate up to 2500 kW for 11 hours daily. About 30 percent of city residents are connected to the system. Their usage is metered, and they pay about 35 Afs ($0.70) per kW. There about 70 solar-powered street lights throughout the city. Many government offices, the university, the hospital, and private citizens operate their own generators.

Outside of Khost City, government offices have their own diesel generators, often provided by a donor. Wealthy citizens or entrepreneurs may run their own generators and sell excess power.

Those without electricity use power sources such as kerosene, gas, and wood. Gas for cooking and lighting is readily available throughout the entire province, but all of the gas is imported from other countries. If a family cannot afford a gas stove and lamp, they will use wood for cooking. The majority use wood for heating.

Transportation

Almost every district is linked to Khost City by an asphalt road. There are 345 km of asphalted road in Khost, of which 120 km of road was newly constructed by the US during the post-Taliban period. Several other sections of poorly maintained road were rehabilitated in the period. The 12 roads that connect Khost with Pakistan, Paktya, and Paktika average around 10,000 vehicles per day. The most important of these is the Khost-Gardez road, which is becoming an important supply route from Pakistan as improvements are completed.

There are 80,000 vehicles in the province. Income in the transportation sector averages around 1 million Afs ($20,000) per month, including the proceeds of 2,500 taxi cars. There are a few government-owned buses in the province, but they are leased and run by private operators. The only bus route runs from Khost City to Nadir Shah Kot and Mando Zai, along the Khost-Gardez road. For the other districts, people rely on taxi stands in the district centers to travel to Khost City.

The more mountainous areas such as Qalander and Spera remain hard to access. Currently, instability in Sabari hinders travel northward to Bak and Zazi Maidan.

Irrigation

Water is generally more abundant in Khost than in most other parts of the country. Canals and underground *karez* systems historically distributed water to fertile agricultural land. However, these systems are difficult and dangerous to maintain. Decades of war have taken their toll on the locals, as the locals were often intentionally targeted by the Soviets. In addition, there is no comprehensive plan for water management and much of the water available is not used wisely. Most irrigation is done inefficiently by flooding fields. Therefore, even when there is good rainfall, the amount of water within the irrigation systems may not be adequate.

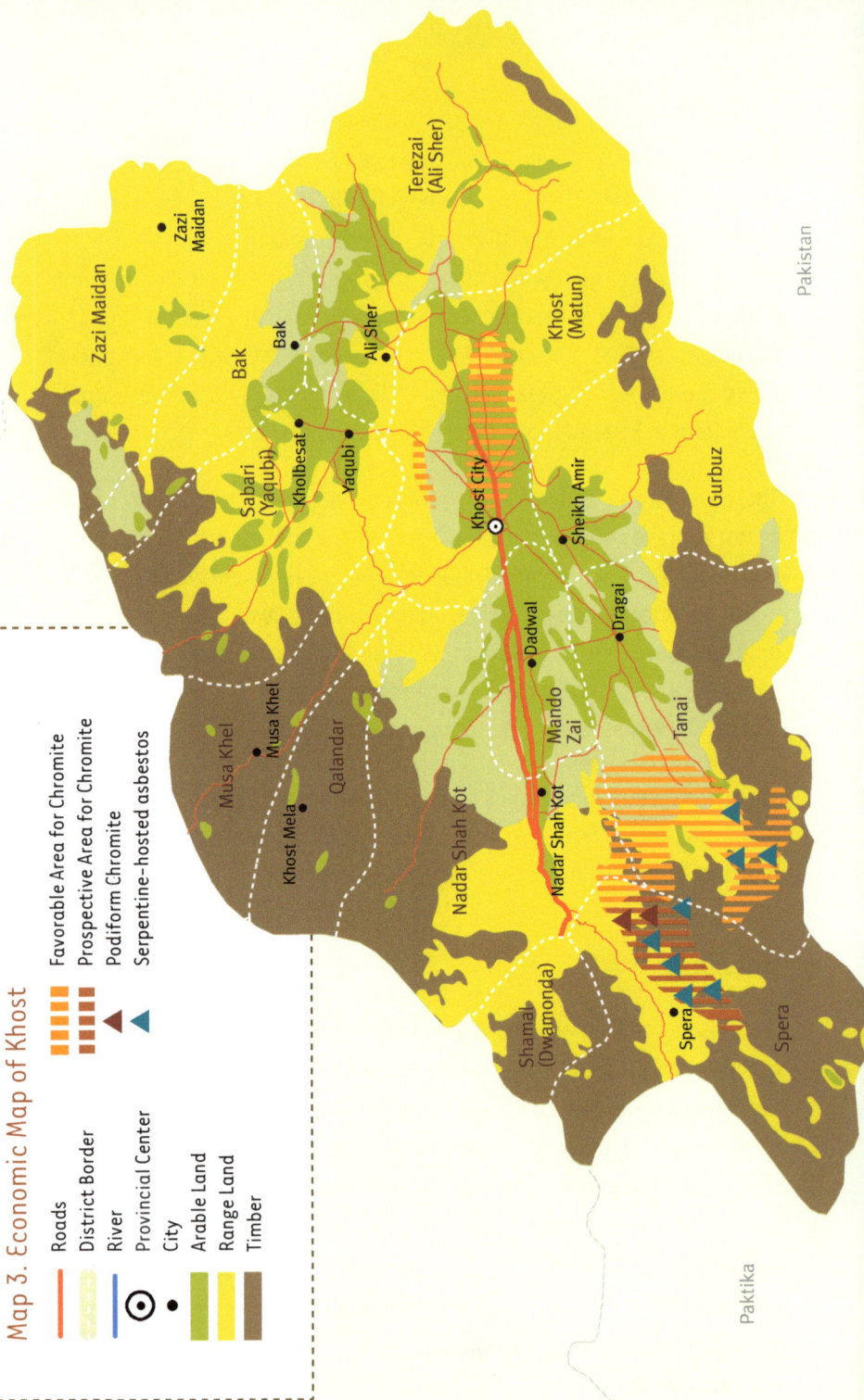

Map 3. Economic Map of Khost

Roads

District Border

River

Provincial Center

City

Arable Land

Range Land

Timber

Favorable Area for Chromite

Prospective Area for Chromite

Podiform Chromite

Serpentine-hosted asbestos

Zazi Maidan

Zazi Maidan

Terezai (Ali Sher)

Bak

Bak

Ali Sher

Khost (Matun)

Sabari (Yaqubi)

Kholbesat

Yaqubi

Khost City

Sheikh Amir

Gurbuz

Musa Khel

Musa Khel

Qalandar

Dadwal

Mando Zai

Dragai

Tanai

Khost Mela

Nadar Shah Kot

Nadar Shah Kot

Shamal (Dwamonda)

Spera

Spera

Pakistan

Paktika

Khost soil is dense clay, so water does not penetrate quickly. People address this problem by slowing down the spring run-off with check dams. Check dams do not entirely stop the flow of water but slow the flow in order to allow water to seep into the earth. They are used throughout Afghanistan.

Telecommunications

Around 70,000 inhabitants of Khost have a mobile phone. AWCC (Afghan Wireless), Roshan, MTN (Areeba), Etisalat, and CDMA all operate in Khost province. AWCC, Roshan, and MTN provide the best coverage, while Etisalat works to expand its coverage into more remote areas.

KEY ECONOMIC SECTORS

Unemployment continues to be a problem in Khost, where many young people go to other countries to find work and send home remittances. Those who stay in Khost usually earn a living in the sectors described in this section.

Agriculture

Khost's land is fertile and the climate is moderate, providing two growing seasons. Water is available although irrigation is inefficient. Major cereal grains include wheat (summer and winter), corn, barley, and rice. Khostis also grow vegetables such as potatoes, cauliflower, okra, carrots, tomatoes, garlic, onions, and lettuce. Farmers in Mando Zai and Khost (Matun) produce apricots, pomegranates, peaches, and chilies. The forests in Zazi Maidan, Spera, Musa Khel, and Qalandar districts are sources of walnuts and apples, but not enough to sell on a large scale.

The amount of surplus food produced by Khost's farmers is small. Most food sold in Khost City is imported from Paksitan. Crops exported to Pakistan in small amounts are sugar cane from Terezai, sesame from Tanai, olives from Musa Khel, and cotton from Terezai and Mando Zai.

Livestock

Usually families keep chickens, goats, sheep, and cows, mostly for their own consumption, but a few to sell in the market. They produce milk, yogurt, and butter for home use. Donkeys are often kept as work animals. Kuchi communities also keep camels and donkeys for transportation. Because there is inadequate grazing land, families need to grow fodder, mainly alfalfa and clover, for their animals.

Veterinary services were established through USAID in 2003 and are now privatized. Services are paid for through fees and government subsidies, but they are still not available to the extent needed in rural areas. Therefore, people often lose animals due to routine and preventable diseases.

Mining

Khost has potential for copper, zinc, and chromite mines. A contract was negotiated with an Afghan firm for extraction of chromite in Tanai and Spera districts, with the potential to produce $6 million per year. However, the mining operation is currently suspended, due to security problems. The future of this project is uncertain.

A major problem with mining in Khost is the lack of power to process the ore on site. Raw material must be shipped outside the country for processing, constraining local profits.

Trade

Khost is on a strategic transit route, and the trade with Pakistan is one of the engines of economic activity in the province. The power of this engine is currently limited, as the Khost-Gardez road has sections that are in disrepair. When construction is completed it is anticipated that the new road will transform the province. The road should become the preferred route for goods shipped between Kabul and Karachi,

Pakistan, as it will be almost 400 km shorter than the current routes through Kandahar or Jalalabad.

Timber

As the population of Khost grows and the productivity of the land does not, some people have turned to illegal timber-cutting to earn a living. Gradually the forests of the province are disappearing. Much of the wood is being transported to Kabul for firewood where it can be sold for two to three times as much as in Khost. Some of the wood is smuggled into Pakistan for lumber. Most of the wood comes from the mountainous areas of Spera, Tanai, Qalandar, Musa Khel, and Shamal.

Small Industries

Small industries are scarce in Khost. Around 20 villages scattered among Shamal, Zazi Maidan, and Tanai districts keep bees for honey. A handful in Terezai, Mando Zai, and Gurbuz produce silk. Mando Zai weaves carpets, while Sabari and Tanai produce jewelry.

TRENDS AND RELEVANT ISSUES

Much of the growth of the economy is attributed to remittances that are sent home from men working abroad. The Khost government website states that 100,000 Khostis are working abroad, mainly in Gulf States or in Europe. It is estimated they contribute $6-7 million each month to the Khost economy.

While some men go abroad to earn funds to send home, others go to earn enough to marry. In Pashtun society, a man must pay the father of a bride a large amount of money, commonly $4,000-$15,000. It is very hard to raise this much money inside Afghanistan.

Provincial officials attend a capacity building workshop. In Khost, USAID puts a premium on the development of capacity building in governance through the Local Governance and Community Development program.

PHOTO BY RAHMATULLAH KAWSAR

Chapter 5
International Organizations and Reconstruction Activities

PROVINCIAL RECONSTRUCTION TEAM

The PRT in Khost is operated by the US Navy. Its leadership team draws from US military and civilian agencies. Military personnel are drawn from active ranks, as well as National Guard and Reserves. The civilian component consists of the US Department of State (DoS), USAID, US Department of Agriculture (USDA), and US Army Corps of Engineers (USACE). The mission of the PRT is to assist the Afghan government in extending its authority.

Most funding for PRT projects comes from USAID and from the US military's CERP funds. In general, the PRT has used CERP funds for infrastructure and agriculture projects. Decisions on allocation of USAID money are usually done at the national level, funding programs in health, education, infrastructure, economic growth, agriculture, and democracy and governance. At the provincial level, USAID field staff direct budgets through the Local Governance and Community Development (LGCD) program. This program is scheduled to end in 2010.

USAID builds the capacity of provincial government offices through LGCD, and the city government through the Municipal Strengthening Program. The PRT has a good working relationship with provincial, district, and municipal officials, as well as most tribal officials. One exception is Sabari, where tribal leaders are uncooperative.

NATIONAL SOLIDARITY PROGRAM

The National Solidarity Program (NSP) is a nationwide, grass-roots development program which places development in the hands of the local population. Community Development Councils (CDCs) prioritize, plan, and implement local development projects that benefit the whole community. It is in its second phase in Khost, which is scheduled to be completed in 2010. The Ministry of Rural Rehabilitation and Development (MRRD) is currently discussing funding of a third phase with donors.

Through its implementer in Khost, the International Rescue Committee (IRC), NSP has worked on more projects than any other program in the province. It has concentrated on the districts of Khost (Matun), Spera, Mando Zai, Tanai, Zazi Maidan, and most of Musa Khel. In these areas, the program has been effective and many CDCs have spent their budgets. Security has been the greatest impediment to implementing NSP in other areas. The most common projects undertaken by NSP so far in Khost have been irrigation, solar panels, flood protection walls, and diversion dams.

PROJECTS AND ACTIVITIES

Electricity

The Khost PRT is currently upgrading the electricity distribution system in Khost City, so that the number of residents with access to the system will increase from its current level of 30 percent to 60 percent. The US military is conducting a hydrological assessment of the southeast region to determine if there are possible hydro-power locations. In 2008, the PRT completed five micro-hydros in Khost and three more in 2009. The NSP is also spreading electricity to the outer districts of the province through small hydro-electric generators and solar lighting. There are no current plans to connect Khost province to the national power grid.

Transportation

As a landlocked country, Afghanistan relies on land routes for its trade, primarily to the Pakistani port of Karachi. Traders will soon have a more direct route with the completion of the 285 km road linking Khost with both the Pakistani border and Paktya's capital, Gardez. USAID has completed the segment from Kabul to Gardez but plans to finish the Khost-Gardez (KG) road in 2009 were delayed. This will connect with the 35 km road from Khost to the Pakistan border paved by CERP. The new route will decrease the journey between Karachi and Kabul by approximately 400 km.

The Khost PRT has allocated $12 million for a provincial civilian airport, expected to be completed in two years. Currently, there is no access to regular air travel for most Khostis. Occasionally, Khost officials are able to fly on planes operated by the US military.

Irrigation

There have been extensive projects in Khost in recent years to improve irrigation. There are many completed and ongoing projects to build dams, flood walls, and canals to control water flow. Many of the projects have been carried out by the PRT through CERP, and several others were part of NSP.

Education

Education for children and adults has been a focus of the donor community in Khost. Donors constructed 18 schools in 2008, with 30 more being built in 2009. Basic Education for Afghans (BEFA) supports over 30 non-traditional schools to educate young adults who missed education during years of war. BEFA is also initiating literacy courses for over 4,500 students, of which more than 3,000 are female. The PRT is also funding combined religious and secular education by building government "Centers of Educational Excellence." Upon completion, there will be one COEE in each district center for primary and middle school, as well as one high school, with dormitories to accommodate students from throughout the province. There are a total of 225 schools serving 174,000 students (40,000 female and 134,000 male). Of these schools, 57 are primary, 15 are middle, and 54 are high schools. There is one teacher training center.

Healthcare

With the World Bank having phased out funding for government health services in the summer of 2009, USAID, WHO and UNICEF are the only sponsors of government health services in Khost. Still, a variety of donors run private health clinics. Although there are under-served areas in the province, approximately 80 percent of people now have access to primary health care.

The PRT is building a new 150-bed hospital. Meanwhile, the Khost University health training system is being upgraded with a new 136-bed teaching hospital, funded by the Afghan government.

An intensive 18-month midwife program trains women at Khost hospital in classes of 30 students. Two classes have graduated. USAID is constructing a new facility with dormitories for this program.

Rule of Law

A nationwide USAID program builds the capacity of the courts through training judges and staff. The pay system for judicial sector officials is currently being reformed at the national level. According to the governor of Khost, the USAID capacity building courses had a positive effect in judiciary.

The Khost PRT constructed a new justice facility, the first of its kind in the country, which it completed and turned over to the Directorate of Justice in January 2009. The facility features a new prison, a court room, offices and personal quarters for lawyers and judges, temporary holding cells, and a mosque.

Table 8: UN Organizations and NGOs in Khost

ABBREVIATION	FULL NAME	MAIN ACTIVITIES
AADA	Agency for Assistance and Development in Afghanistan	Health Services
APA	Afghanistan Planning Agency	Humanitarian Assistance
BEFA	Basic Education for Afghans	Education
CARE	CARE	Education
DHSA	Development and Humanitarian Services for Afghanistan	Education
GTZ	German Technical Cooperation	Economic Development, Water, Energy
HNI	Health Network International	Health Services
IMC	International Medical Corps (IMC)	Health Services
IRC	International Rescue Committee	Community Development
ROW	Rehabilitation Organization for Women	Community Development for Women
TLO	Tribal Liaison Office	Conflict Resolution, Livelihood Improvement
UNHCR	United Nation High Commissioner for Refugees	Health Services, Infrastructure, Capacity Building
UNAMA	United Nation Assistance Mission in Afghanistan	Governance, Donor Coordination
WFP	World Food Program	Humanitarian Food Aid

Peace Message Radio, shown here, is the first independent radio in Khost. Due to low literacy rates and the expense of televisions, radio is the most popular form of media and an important source of national news.

PHOTO BY RAHMATULLAH KAWSAR

Chapter 6
Information and Influence

Most Khostis have radios, making the radio the most important conduit of information in the province. However, mullahs continue to be an important source of information both during Friday prayer and outside the mosque.

The mullahs' influence is exercised through their sermons. There is no separation of mosque and state in Afghanistan. All laws must be in line with Islamic principles. Thus, the opinions of mullahs concerning the consistency of state law with religious law are important. While some mullahs are educated, others are uneducated, like many of their followers. They can be a speedy conduit for misinformation, and even the strangest rumors will often be believed. Since mullahs are so influential, it is important to reach out to them either directly or through their hierarchy, such as through the Directorate of Hajj and Religious Affairs.

MEDIA ACTIVITY AND INFLUENCE

At one time there was only a state-run radio station in Khost, which continues to operate and deliver official government messages from the Directorate of Information and Culture.

Since 2004, Khost University has operated an independent radio station, **Zwan Ghagh**, which broadcasts seven hours per day. The facilities for the radio were donated to the university by the Khost PRT. The radio equipment and the first six months of operating costs were supplied by USAID. Since then, the operations have been funded by a combination of Afghan government funding and commercial revenue. There are now two more private radio stations, **Sole Paigham** and **Walas Ghagh**, whose messages are shaped by their owners and boards of directors. Khost's residents also receive broadcasts from national TV stations such as **Tolo, Lemar, Ariana,** and **Shamshad**.

Radio is much more prevalent than television and is most often the best way to get out a message to the mostly illiterate population. However, when Khostis want to check the accuracy of their local radio stations, they usually turn to the international shortwave broadcasts of the BBC and VOA.

A number of print media organizations have also emerged, but only two appear regularly: *Paiwastoon*, a monthly, and *Walas Hila*, a weekly. This media tends to be a combination of news, entertainment, art, history, health tips, and poetry. The educated elite of Khost residents who read these judge their current quality to be low, but they are hopeful that these organizations will improve.

Table 9: Radio and Television Stations in Khost

RADIO/TV NAME	HEAD OF THE RADIO/TV	CELL PHONE
Sole Paigham (Peace Message Radio)	Zahid Shah Angar	0799-406-167
Walas Ghagh (Voice of the Nation)	Bismillah Haqmal	0707-004-545
Zwan Ghagh (Youth Voice Radio at Khost University)	Ostaz Wahidi	0700-074-026
Khost Radio and TV (Radio Television Afghanistan – Ministry of Information and Culture)	Saki Sarwar Meakhail	0799-136-637

The Afghan National Army displays the weapons and equipment it has seized from insurgents. The ANA is considered the most functional Afghan security institution, and is generally well regarded.

PHOTO BY FRANCES FIERST

Chapter 7
The Big Issues

THE HAQQANI NETWORK, THE TALIBAN, AND THE HIG

The former mujahedin leader Jalaludin Haqqani of the Zadran tribe and his son Sirajuddin lead a network of insurgents and terrorists that dominates anti-government activity in Khost. The network is allied with the Taliban and relies on them for bases in Pakistan near the border with Khost, as well as other support. Jalauddin has a long-standing relationship with Pakistani ISI and al-Qaeda from his days fighting against the Communist government. In addition, the Haqqani family is strongly affiliated with several traditionalist madrassas in the border region.

Beyond its frequent attacks in Khost province, the Haqqani Network has shown its ability to operate in Kabul. It is believed to have organized the assault on the Serena Hotel in January 2008, as well as the assassination attempt against President Karzai in April in conjunction with the Hezb-e-Islami Gulbuddin (HIG) terrorist network. HIG and the Taliban are also responsible for some attacks within Khost, but they do not match the presence of the Haqqani Network. The Haqqani Network is most active in Spera and the districts of the Zadran Arc, frequently attacking Afghan and coalition forces on the highway between Khost and Gardez.

Map 4. Conflict Map of Khost

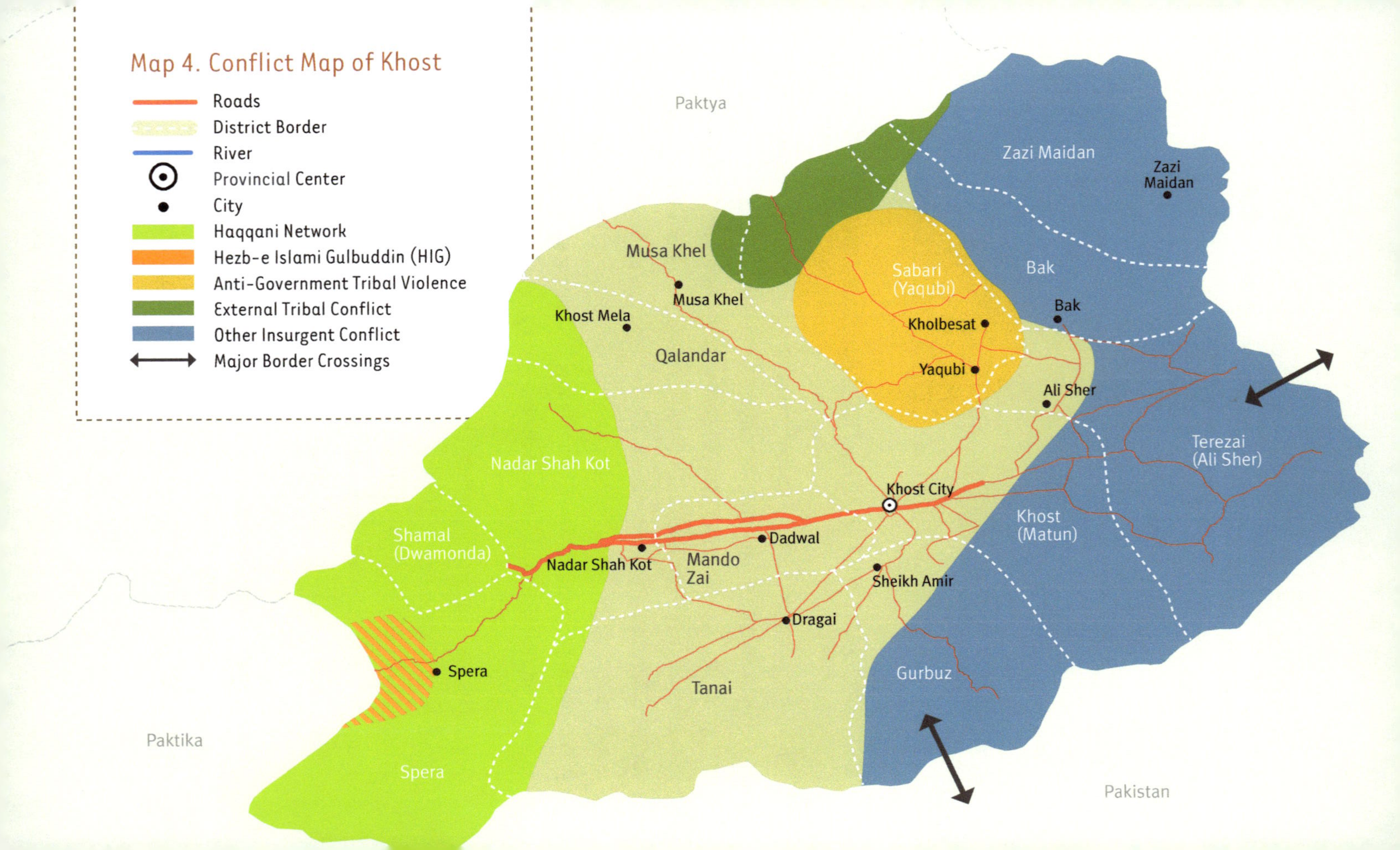
Roads
District Border
River
Provincial Center
City
Haqqani Network
Hezb-e Islami Gulbuddin (HIG)
Anti-Government Tribal Violence
External Tribal Conflict
Other Insurgent Conflict
Major Border Crossings
Paktya
Paktika
Pakistan
Zazi Maidan
Zazi Maidan
Bak
Bak
Sabari (Yaqubi)
Kholbesat
Yaqubi
Ali Sher
Terezai (Ali Sher)
Khost City
Khost (Matun)
Musa Khel
Musa Khel
Khost Mela
Qalandar
Nadar Shah Kot
Nadar Shah Kot
Dadwal
Mando Zai
Sheikh Amir
Dragai
Tanai
Gurbuz
Shamal (Dwamonda)
Spera
Spera

LAND DISPUTES

One of the most devastating weaknesses of the current government in Afghanistan is its inability to provide dispute resolution. This manifests itself in many ways, and one of the most important is the large number of outstanding cases over conflicting land claims.

As waves of people fled from the area in the last three decades, others moved onto their land. When the previous occupants returned, they found new people farming the land they had left behind. Government officials have often awarded land to people who supported them politically, without regard for proper titles. Often the title to one piece of land has been issued to more than one person.

An area just west of Khost City was designated to be distributed to government officials and the ANA, as well as to disadvantaged people such as widows and the poor. The program caused civil unrest because the land is valuable and in a desirable location. In the fall of 2008, there was a five-day protest outside of the mayor's office because these plots of land had not yet been distributed. By early 2009, locals believed that more than half of the 1,200 plots had been given to close relatives of the governor.

Khostis have no confidence in the ability of the judicial system or any other part of the government to resolve land disputes. This aspect of government is viewed as especially corrupt, and parties to a dispute will not comply with government directives. With no reliable or respected justice system in place, families and tribes argue continually over conflicting claims, and the arguments escalate to violence and blood feuds.

The Karzai government's approach to resolving land disputes stands in stark contrast to their resolution during the Taliban regime. People often took land disputes to the Taliban, who were seen as impartial judges. The judgments were made according to Sharia law, and the parties to the dispute accepted the outcome. Decisions were made quickly and

were free of government bribes and delays. Despite all the improvements since the end of the Taliban regime, this deficiency of the current
government is one major reason that some people view the Taliban
government with nostalgia.

REFUGEE RETURNS

In the post-Taliban era, it is estimated that over 12,000 families who
had left Afghanistan have returned to Khost province. Only about 200 of
these returned through a UN High Commissioner for Refugees (UNHCR)
program which provides funds and other assistance to returnees. Due
to the difficulty in finding a place for all the returning refugees, a new
township of Qalamwal was created on land near Forward Operating
Base Salerno. However, neighbors came forward claiming the land as
their private property. This issue has prevented refugees from settling
on the land. As of publication, the dispute remains unresolved.

In a separate land dispute, an area just west of Khost City was designated to be distributed to government officials and ANA, as well as
to disadvantaged people such as widows and the poor. However, the
program has caused civil unrest because the land is valuable and in
a desirable location. In the fall of 2008, there was a five-day protest
outside of the mayor's office because these plots of land had not yet
been distributed. By early 2009, more than half of the 1,200 plots had
been given away.

Unfortunately, this land is where some refugees settled when they were
denied plots in Qalamwal. Many refugees were squatting and they
now face eviction. Government officials say they will only allow those
who are documented with UNHCR to stay, which represents a small
percentage of all the squatters. In the meantime, there is little oversight

as to how the land is being distributed, and there are many accusations of corruption. Government officials are accused of giving the land to family and friends, and not to the disadvantaged. In the meantime, the local government is using this program as a means to forcibly remove undocumented refugees.

In late 2008, Pakistani refugees from the Kurram Agency fled across the border into Afghanistan to escape sectarian violence between Sunni and Shia. Unofficial documents suggest around 200 such families live in Zazi Maidan and Terezai.

The Afghan government is continuing to address addresses these issues through the Ministry of Refugees and the Disaster Management Committee. The PRT has funded some humanitarian assistance through military and USAID funds, but the main international actors have been UNHCR, UNICEF, and WFP. So far, the refugee issue has not significantly affected the work of the PRT, and the issue remains a low-level threat to security.

OPIUM GROWTH AND TRAFFICKING

The UN Office of Drugs and Crime (UNODC) reports that Khost was poppy-free during the 2007 fall planting season, improving from its mark of 133 hectares planted in 2006. In 2008, Khost received $1,000,000 from the Good Performers Initiative because the province was deemed poppy free. With the money from this fund the governor procured improved seed and fertilizers to distribute to the farmers. Khost received funds through this program again in 2009. It is difficult to pinpoint the cause of the improvement, but the provincial government was engaged in several actions to make this possible. The Directorate of Counternarcotics at the provincial level worked with religious leaders to discourage farmers from growing poppy.

This directorate also worked closely with the Directorate of Sports to present a public information campaign at sporting events to discourage the planting of poppy. Drug smuggling is not believed to be a significant activity in Khost.

WEAPONS SMUGGLING

In the past, Khost has been a major route for smuggling weapons. During Communist rule, weapons were brought into the country from Pakistan for use by the mujahedin, especially those from Miram Shah in North Waziristan. After the Soviets withdrew, the surplus of weapons was smuggled from Afghanistan back to Pakistan. These same well-known infiltration routes are now believed to be in use by the Taliban to bring weapons and explosives from Pakistan.

RELATIONS WITH PAKISTAN

During the period of Communist rule, opponents of the Communists in Khost emigrated to Pakistan. Many people of Khost already maintained strong family ties with Pakistanis across the border, and these were strengthened by their interactions during that period. Today, people continue to move freely across the border as they interact with the various branches of their families. Some Khostis still live in Pakistan and are potential recruits for anti-government forces.

Criminals from each country are known to find refuge easily on the other side of the border. Khost residents strongly believe that anti-Afghan forces maintain bases in Pakistan and infiltrate Afghanistan's territory regularly, especially from bases in the Miram Shah and Wazirsitan areas.

GOVERNMENT LEGITIMACY

The perceived legitimacy of the central government is on a downward trend in the estimation of most Khost residents. Many cite the government's inability to address the high rate of unemployment among youth. Others believe there is wide-scale embezzlement and bribery at the provincial and central levels of government. In 2007, after the end of Pattan's time as governor, Afghanistan's attorney general came to Khost to investigate corruption in the provincial government. Several officials, including directors from various ministries, were taken into custody, but were later found not guilty at trial.

Throughout the country there are highly-publicized cases of corruption that contribute to the mistrust between the people and their government. People are especially upset that criminals are able to pay bribes to the government to avoid punishment.

Corruption is particularly bad in and around Khost City. With the huge influx of development and assistance money, there are lots of opportunities for skimming funds from contracts and grants. Corruption also occurs in the districts, because the military and aid agencies are unable to visit them often enough to monitor projects. The quality of materials and construction is often compromised as funds are redirected for personal enrichment. In some cases the fraud is so great that the building is never built, and a falsified report is submitted to the donor agency.

The people who are supposed to receive aid know that corruption is blocking the development projects they have been anticipating. Whether the funds for the project are controlled by the government or an outside organization, this malfeasance destroys the credibility of the provincial government.

Most Khostis are conservative Sunnis Muslims, praying five times a day and attending mosques such as this one. No outsider should show disrespect toward the religion.

PHOTO BY SABAWOON HANAN

APPENDICES

TIMELINE OF KEY EVENTS

2001: After the US invasion, brothers Pacha Khan Zadran and Kamal Khan Zadran take control of Paktya and Khost, respectively.

2002: Hakim Tanaiwal, Afghan exile and sociology teacher, is appointed to replace Kamal as governor, becoming the first Karzai appointee to lead the province. Khost is secure and peaceful during his two years in office.

2004: Merajuddin Pattan succeeds Tanaiwal as governor. He builds strong ties between the government and the PRT, but his two years in power are marred by poor management and the lack of available reconstruction funds.

2006: Arsala Jamal succeeds Pattan as governor. His time in office sees a dramatic increase in funding for projects, but he is dogged by accusations of corruption.

2006: Afghan and US forces are stationed together in district government centers, which become heavily fortified. The intent is for US forces to train ANSF, as well as to be a visible sign of security in outlying areas.

2007: Afghan University in Peshawar, Pakistan, relocates to Khost, and becomes a major center of higher learning in Afghanistan.

2008: Several attacks on district government centers prompt Afghan and US officials to relocate US forces to separate force protection centers. The goal is to continue to keep a security presence in the area, without drawing fire upon district government facilities.

2008: Construction begins on the Khost-Gardez road, which will become Afghanistan's shortest transit route from Kabul to the nearest port in Karachi, Pakistan.

2009: Hamidullah Qalandarzoi, an experienced administrator within the Karzai administration in Kabul, is appointed to replace Jamal as governor; his time as governor is short-lived, however, and he leaves office amid accusations of incompetence.

COMMON COMPLIMENTS OF US FORCES IN SOUTHEASTERN AFGHANISTAN

- Afghans compliment US forces for bringing security.

- Afghans believe US forces do not steal from people – unlike local security forces and the central government – and that they try to be honest.

- Afghans respect international forces for leaving their families to come and help them.

- Afghans compliment the US forces' work ethic.

- Afghans appreciate reconstruction projects, such as new roads, that change their lives for the better after decades of war.

COMMON COMPLAINTS OF US FORCES IN SOUTHEASTERN AFGHANISTAN

- US troops conduct military operations at night without coordinating them with the local or central government.

- US operations sometimes take the lives of civilians and innocent people.

- US forces carry out unwarranted house searches and detentions. These violate the sanctity of the home. These acts have driven a segment of the population who might otherwise have sided with the government to support the anti-government forces.

- US forces do not work earnestly for security. They are rich and powerful, so they could easily destroy the Taliban.

- US forces lack respect for culture and traditions. This includes a lack of respect and understanding of the way women should be treated by foreign troops.

- US forces use dishonest informers and interpreters, who have their own agendas, for their intelligence gathering.

- Too much international aid goes to wealthy or corrupt individuals.

Table 10: Tribal Leaders in Khost

DISTRICT NAME	TRIBAL LEADER NAME	TRIBE NAME
Shamal/Nadir Shah Kot	Haji Wali	Zadran
Shamal/Nadir Shah Kot	Haji Shirgul	Zadran
Shamal/Nadir Shah Kot	Haji Sakhi Jan	Zadran
Shamal/Nadir Shah Kot	Shir Nawaz Khan	Zadran
Shamal/Nadir Shah Kot	Haji Nazim	Zadran
Terezai	Haji Skhi	Terezai
Terezai	Mualem Mohammad Deen,	Terezai
Terezai	Haji Hakeem Shah	Terezai
Terezai	Mualem Rahmat Shah	Terezai
Terezai	Ali Gul	Terezai
Sabari	Mir Zaman Sabari	Sabari
Sabari	Mohammad Ali	Sabari
Sabari	Haji Sharbati	Sabari
Sabari	Haji Madi Gul	Sabari
Sabari	Gul Rahim	Sabari
Gurbuz	Shaha Khan	Waziri
Gurbuz	Mawla Khan	Waziri
Gurbuz	Gul Ahmas Khan	Waziri
Gurbuz	Nawab Khan	Waziri
Gurbuz	Zahiduddeen	Waziri
Gurbuz	Muzboot	Waziri
Khost (Matun)	Abdul Qayum Khan	Lakan
Khost (Matun)	Sakhi Jan Sarhadi	Lakan
Khost (Matun)	Zabet Zahid	Lakan
Khost (Matun)	Shah Pur	Lakan
Khost (Matun)	Haji Jahangul	Lakan
Musa Khel	Wazir Mangal	Mangal
Musa Khel	Mehrabat Khan	Mangal
Musa Khel	Haji Shahrak Gul	Mangal
Musa Khel	Musa Jan Mangal	Mangal
Musa Khel	Zabet Aminjan	Mangal

DISTRICT NAME	TRIBAL LEADER NAME	TRIBE NAME
Musa Khel	Mehrbaz Khan	Ismail Khel
Musa Khel	Mir Wali Khan	Ismail Khel
Musa Khel	Haji Shahbaz Khan	Ismail Khel
Musa Khel	Haji Noor Afzal	Ismail Khel
Musa Khel	Engineer Mazar	Ismail Khel
Khost (Matun)	Rahmatgul	These are unofficial leaders in the urban centers and are not tribal leaders as such.
Khost (Matun)	Mullah Abdul Qudus	
Khost (Matun)	Mohmmad Azim Khan	
Khost (Matun)	Sharifullah	
Khost (Matun)	Ghafrullah	
Khost (Matun)	Yaqut	
Tanai	Haji Malis	Tanai
Tanai	Haji Ali Khan	Tanai
Tanai	Haji Mailan	Tanai
Tanai	Haji Samswar Khan	Tanai
Tanai	Haji Mirbadad	Tanai
Khost (Matun)	Ghafar Noorzai	Matun
Khost (Matun)	Saila Khan	Matun
Khost (Matun)	Sayed Habib Shah	Matun
Khost (Matun)	Haji Qudoos	Matun
Khost (Matun)	Muftai Habiburrehman (mullah)	Matun
Bak	Gul Rahman	Babakar Khel
Bak	Najibullah	Babakar Khel
Bak	Shahzad	Babakar Khel
Bak	Khialai Gul	Babakar Khel
Different Districts of Khost	Haji Qamari	Kuchi (Nomads)
Different Districts of Khost	Haji Muslim	Kuchi (Nomads)
Different Districts of Khost	Peeri Kuchi	Kuchi (Nomads)
Different Districts of Khost	Toor Kuchi	Kuchi (Nomads)
Different Districts of Khost	Khanagi	Kuchi (Nomads)
Different Districts of Khost	Haji Mohammad Raheem	Kuchi (Nomads)

DAY IN THE LIFE OF A RURAL KHOSTI

The life of a rural Khosti begins early in the morning with the Imam's call for the first prayer of the day one hour before sunrise. Men of the family get up, wash, and go to their village mosque. Young boys take the cows to the fields or go to school. Women pray at home, start a fire, and prepare breakfast. Breakfast in the house of a poor man is tea mixed with milk and bread; a wealthier man will have milk, cheese, homemade butter, and local pastries. After breakfast, men go to the field or other work. Women stay at home or go help the men in the field. A typical lunch in Khost is rice and cereal with cooked vegetables, and is typically accompanied with yogurt and slices of onion or other kinds of fresh vegetables from the fields. After lunch, everyone prays in the afternoon and then takes a nap. When they wake up, they have green tea and work again in the field. Next is the third prayer of the day, when men gather in front of mosques or under the shade of a tree and catch up on the happenings from the day before. Children go to the mosque to study the Holy Koran and other religious books with the Imam. Women milk the animals and process cheese, butter, and yogurt in the cool of late afternoon. The fourth prayer of the day takes place before dinner, and when it is complete everyone rushes home to eat dinner as a family. After dinner, the family talks about the day's events and discusses the plan for the next day. Then the final prayer of the day is completed and everyone goes to sleep. During the summer, people sleep outside on their roofs.

FURTHER READING AND SOURCES

Books

- NATO, *ISAF PRT Handbook*, 3rd Ed. February 2007.

- Sarah Chayes, *The Punishment of Virtue: Inside Afghanistan After the Taliban*, New York: Penguin Press, 2006.

- Steve Coll, *Ghost Wars: The Secret History of the CIA, Afghanistan, and Bin Laden, From the Soviet Invasion to September 10, 2001*, New York: Penguin Press, 2004.

- Louis Dupree, *Afghanistan,* Princeton: Princeton University Press, 1979.

- Edward R. Girardet, *Afghanistan*: The Soviet War, New Delhi, India: Selectbook Service Syndicate, 1985.

- Edward Girardet and Jonathan Walter, *Afghanistan: Essential Field Guides to Humanitarian and Conflict Zones*, CROSSLINES Publication Ltd, 1998 and 2004.

- Larry Goodson, *Afghanistan's Endless War: State Failure, Regional Politics, and the Rise of the Taliban*, Seattle: University of Washington Press, 2001.

- Michael Griffin, *Reaping the Whirlwind: The Taliban Movement in Afghanistan*, London: Pluto Press, 2001.

- Ben Macintyre, *The Man Who Would Be King: The First American in Afghanistan*, New York: Farrar, Straus and Giroux, 2005.

- Greg Mortenson, *Three Cups of Tea: One Man's Mission to Promote Peace ... One School at a Time*, New York: Penguin Books, 2006. (Excellent understanding of how to succeed with the people and culture)

- Sean Naylor, *Not a Good Day to Die: The Untold Story of Operation Anaconda*, London: Penquin/Michael Joseph, 2005.

- Ahmed Rashid, *Descent into Chaos: The United States and the Future of Nation Building in Afghanistan, Pakistan, and Central Asia*, New York: Viking Press, 2008.

- Ahmed Rashid, *Taliban: Militant Islam, Oil and Fundamentalism in Central Asia*, New Haven: Yale University Press, 2000.

- Barnett Rubin, *The Fragmentation of Afghanistan*, New Haven: Yale University Press, 2001.

Articles

- Hamed Karzai, *The Afghanistan National Development Strategy*, 2006, *www.reliefweb.int/rw/RWFiles2006.nsf/ dbc12f058effd2dac125749600457fd4/c125723c004042d7c12573aa0 0474d8b/$FILE/unama-afg-30jan2.pdf*

- G.H. Orris and J.D. Bliss (eds), *Mines and Mineral Occurrences of Afghanistan*, open-file report 02-110, US Geological Survey, US Department of the Interior, 2002.

- Barnett Rubin, "Afghanistan's Uncertain Transition from Turmoil to Normalcy," *Council Special Report*, No. 12, March 2007.

- Wilder, Andrew. "Cops or Robbers: The Struggle to Reform the Afghan National Police," *Afghan Research and Evaluation Unit*, July 2007, *www.areu.org.af/index php?option=com_docman&task=doc_download&gid=523*

Web Sites

- Afghanistan Research and Evaluation Unit (publishes the *Afghanistan A to Z guide*), *www.areu.org.af/index.php?option=com_frontpage&Itemid=25*

- Afghanistan Information Management Services, *www.aims.org.af*

- Afghanistan Online (Links to Official IRA and embassy websites), *www.afghan-web.com/politics*

- Naval Postgraduate School Program for Culture and Conflict Studies, *www.nps.edu/Programs/CCS/index.html*

- USAID, *www.usaid.gov/locations/asia/countries/afghanistan*

- Afghanistan Central Statistics Office, *www.cso-af.net*

- Khost City website (in Pashto), *khost.gov.af*

- Global Security, *www.globalsecurity.org*

- Afghanistan Ministry of Rural Rehabilitation and Development, *www.mrrd.gov.af*

www.ingramcontent.com/pod-product-compliance
Lightning Source LLC
Chambersburg PA
CBHW040128270326
41927CB00001B/24